ROKEBY PARK PRIMARY SCHOOL

Farming Communities

Small mixed farms that grew enough crops and raised enough animals to supply the needs of the local community have now mostly been replaced by larger more productive farming businesses, but a few still remain.

WAYS OF LIFE

Farming Communities

BY BRIAN WILLIAMS

Illustrated by Gwen Green

CHERRYTREE BOOKS

Picture credits: Australian Overseas Information Service p30, p31; Farming Information Centre p7 (bottom); Finnish Tourist Board p38 (top); Frank Lane Picture Agency p26, p28 (bottom); Hutchison Library p2, p7 (top), p8, p9, p14, p28 (top), p29, p32, p33, p34 (right), p36, p37, p38 (centre), p39, p40, p41, p42, p43, p44, p47.

A Cherrytree Book

Designed and produced by
AS Publishing

First published 1992
by Cherrytree Press Ltd
a subsidiary of
The Chivers Company Ltd
Windsor Bridge Road
Bath, Avon BA2 3AX

Copyright © Cherrytree Press Ltd 1992

British Library Cataloguing in Publication Data
Williams, Brian
   Farming Communities.—(Ways of Life Series)
   I. Title II. Green, Gwen III. Series
   307.7

   ISBN 0-7451-5157-4

Printed and bound in Italy by L.E.G.O. s.p.a., Vicenza

All rights reserved. No part of this publication may be reproduced, stored in a retrieval system, or transmitted, in any form or by any means without the prior permission in writing of the publisher, nor be otherwise circulated in any form of binding or cover other than that in which it is published and without a similar condition including this condition being imposed on the subsequent purchaser.

Contents

THE KEY TO CIVILIZATION 6

THE BUSINESS OF FARMING 10

FARMERS OF LONG AGO 16

    The Middle Ages 18
    Farmers of the New World 20
    Towards Today 24

FARMING TODAY 25

    Prairie Grain Growers 26
    Home on the Range 28
    Farmers of Australasia 30
    Surviving in Asia 32
    Peasant Farmers of the Andes 34
    Subsistence in Africa 36
    Cattle Herders of Africa 37
    Nomadic Herders 38
    Communes and Collectives 40

FARMING IN THE MODERN WORLD 43

GLOSSARY 46

INDEX 48

The Key to Civilization

Farming is the world's most important industry. Farmers all over the world produce more and more food every year. Yet two thirds of the world's people are undernourished.

The first farming communities lived about 10,000 years ago in the Middle East. There, people first learned how to plant and harvest wild wheat. It was a tremendous step forward for humanity, and the key to civilization. People no longer had to wander, hunting and gathering their food. They could stay in one place, and build permanent homes. In time, they learned how to *domesticate* and *breed* wild sheep and goats, and later pigs and cattle.

Farmers who grew more food than their own family could eat were able to exchange the extra for other goods or produce, and this helped the development of trade. Farming communities made laws to govern themselves. They held feasts to celebrate good harvests, and learned the wisdom of storing food for use in a lean season.

Opposite: The first farmers planted wild wheat, and harvested the grain with simple hand tools. Everyone helped bring in the harvest.

A Chinese farm today. In much of the world, farm methods have not changed greatly for hundreds of years.

Modern factory farming is efficient. It gives us cheaper food, but many people would prefer to pay a little more so that farm animals like these caged battery hens can lead more natural lives.

☐ Leaving the land

Until about 100 years ago, most people grew at least some of their own food. Then, as countries became industrialized, more and more people left the countryside. They moved to towns to work in factories. These workers had to buy all their food. Farmers who remained in the countryside had to produce enough food to feed them, so farms had to become more productive.

Below: In Asia farmers create extra cropland by terracing hillsides. Here in China farmers plant out young rice plants in a flooded field.

☐ Farming today

During this century, ever more people have made their homes in towns. In 1919, for example, some 35 out of every 100 Americans lived on the land. The United States was a nation of farm communities. Today in the United States fewer than three people in 100 work on a farm. Yet American farmers produce more food than ever before.

In Europe until the 1950s many farms were small. The farmer kept a few pigs, some dairy cows, chickens and ducks in the yard, and tended small fields planted with wheat and vegetables. Now those small farms have mostly been swallowed up by large farms, where huge fields are harvested by machines. Animals may be reared by *intensive* methods on factory farms.

Summer
Summer is the growing season for crops and weeds – and the eating season for pests. Farmers use weedkillers and pesticides, taking care not to harm the soil, plants or farm animals. The animals graze and grow fat and the crops ripen.

Autumn
Harvest time is the busiest season of the year, when traditionally everyone helped to gather in crops before bad weather spoiled them. Cattle are sent to market. Pigs are sent later in the year.

Winter
Animals are fed on hay gathered earlier in the year and brought into sheds in bad weather. Farm equipment is serviced, repaired or replaced. Farmers catch up with the paperwork and plans for the following year.

Harvest festival
People take gifts of food to church for special harvest services. Even town churches hold harvest festivals. Children help decorate the church with sheaves of corn and displays of food. People make small figures called corn dollies from wheat straw. Once these had a magical significance, but today they are mostly sold to tourists.

Harvest suppers
Harvest suppers are still held in many country districts. Everyone enjoys a hearty meal to celebrate the bounty of the harvest.

Thanksgiving
Americans celebrate Thanksgiving Day in memory of the first successful harvest gathered by the Pilgrims in the autumn of 1621. The first settlers in Massachusetts would have starved without the help of friendly Indians, who taught them how to plant beans and corn.

Corn goddess
In Europe people believed that it was bad luck to be seen by the corn goddess, whose home was the cornfields. So they cut the last few stalks very carefully, covering their faces so that the corn goddess could not recognize them.

Corn dollies

Harvest moon
The harvest moon is the full moon seen around the autumn equinox, about September 23 in the northern hemisphere. For several nights, the moon shines so brightly that farmers in northern Europe and Canada can work late into the night to bring in the harvest. In Australia the harvest moon shines during the month of March.

Rice harvest
In Asia, people celebrate the rice harvests. They bake special rice and coconut cakes to eat.

Sugar cane harvest
In Jamaica, sugar cane cutters celebrate the cutting of the ripe cane.

Pineapple harvest
In the Amazon region of South America, the Indians celebrate when pineapples, cassava and other crops are harvested.

Farmers bring horses, cattle, sheep and pigs to town and sell them at *auction*. They also come to buy, casting a critical eye over each animal as it is led round the sale ring. The auctioneer conducts the selling so fast that outsiders cannot follow what is going on, but the regulars make themselves understood with nods and gestures. *Grain* and other products are also auctioned.

Above: This farmer grows only bananas. Some countries, like Grenada in the Caribbean, rely on one or two cash crops, such as bananas. A banana company buys the whole crop.

Above right: Prize bull and proud handler. Agricultural shows and fairs are fun for farmers and for the public who come from the town for a taste of country living.

Many small towns still have livestock and produce markets. In Africa, Asia and South America farmers and their families sell their produce on the street. They spread out their fruit, eggs, herbs and other goods for passers-by to inspect. Haggling (bargaining) over the price is enjoyed by buyer and seller.

☐ **Going to the fair**
Most counties hold an annual fair either in a permanent or temporary fairground. This is an opportunity for everyone to show off. Farmers bring the best of their animals to be judged in competitions for each breed. Samples of fruit and vegetables and other crops are laid out to be judged by experts and admired by all.

There are horse races and horse shows, and other competitive sporting events for children. There are roller coasters, big wheels, merry-go-rounds and shooting galleries. There are fast food stands selling hamburgers, pizzas and popcorn, ice-creams and candy floss. All through the day bands play and the local police force or fire brigade lay on displays.

THRILLS AND SKILLS

Farming communities enjoy entertainments that allow people to show off their skills.

Barbecues
Eating food cooked on an open fire outdoors was normal for people the world over until modern times. Barbecues are still popular with *ranch* and other farming peoples.

Barn dances
These 'square dances' with a host to call out the sequence of moves for the dancers to make were traditional get-togethers eagerly awaited by the farm communities of the 1800s. They gave people a chance to dress up, to meet neighbours they might not have seen for months, and to make new friends. Country music and country dances are still popular today.

Rodeo
The rodeo gives everyone a chance to admire the roughriding skills of broncobusters and steer-ropers. At a rodeo, riders try to ride bulls and unschooled horses for fun, and there are wagon races.

Sheepdog trials
In some European countries dogs are trained to look after flocks of sheep. In a sheepdog trial, shepherds and their dogs compete in driving sheep around a test course. The dog responds to the whistles and calls of its master. Together they make a team.

Ploughing for prizes
Farmers from about 30 countries attend a ploughing competition held in Ireland each year. Competitors are judged on at least 20 aspects of the job.

Horses for pleasure
Although working horses are not seen often on farms nowadays, many farm people enjoy horseriding. Horse shows and races are popular all over the world. In some communities people still dress up to hunt foxes with horns and hounds.

Farmers of Long Ago

Farming allowed people to stay in one place and build a settled community. Finding food no longer took up all people's time. They were able to develop skills in metalworking and pottery, to make new tools and build homes for themselves and temples to their gods.

Egypt is a hot, dry country. Through it runs the River Nile. Every year, in ancient times, the river would flood. For three months, the valley was inundated with water.

As soon as the flood was over, the farmers would plough their fields and sow their seed. Before the next flood, there would be time to harvest three plantings. To extend the amount of farmland, the Egyptians irrigated their fields. They dug ditches from the river and filled them with water by means of a *shaduf*.

Teams of long-horned oxen pulled the ploughs and afterwards helped to trample the seed which was sown by hand. Crops included wheat and barley for making bread, vegetables and fruit, and flax for making clothes. Beer was made from barley and wine from grapes.

As well as crops, the Egyptians raised cattle, pigs, sheep, goats, ducks, geese and other water birds. There was not much grazing land, so the animals were often fed and fattened in their stalls.

☐ **Slaves and women**
The men who tended the fields and the animals were members of the family, workers paid in kind, or slaves owned by the farmer. The women stayed at home to look after the home and children, to work at weaving and to grind the corn to make flour. They had equal status with their husbands and many owned their own properties.

Farmers took their surplus food to market, *bartering* it for goods of similar value – they did not use money.

Irrigation in ancient Egypt.

Rice planting in ancient China.

Shepherds in ancient Greece.

Egypt was a highly organized society, with virtually every aspect of life controlled by the *pharaoh* and his officials. They kept records of the amount of food a farmer produced and collected taxes. Each farmer had to give a proportion of his produce to fund the army and the priesthood.

☐ Feeding China's thousands

Even in ancient times China had a teeming population with not much good farmland. The peasants made use of every bit of land. They terraced hillsides, irrigated dry areas, and built huge earthworks to prevent floods. They grew wheat, millet, maize and soya in the north and rice in the south. Unable to keep up with demand for their crops, from the nobles and warlords, the peasants often went hungry themselves. Just as the emperor had total power over the country, a father had total power over his family. Women worked but had little say in the running of their homes.

☐ Working women of Greece

The Greeks were skilled farmers. Very little of their rocky land was suitable for growing crops, but they grew barley and wheat. There was little pasture, but they raised sheep and goats. Grapes and olives grew well. Their tools were mostly made of wood and they used oxen, and in some places horses, to work their farms. The men of the family worked on the farm, the women in the home and on the farm. Poor women were more independent than the rich who had slaves to do their work. They might take the farm produce to market and sell it on their own stalls.

☐ Farmers – the might of Rome

The greatest empire the world has ever known originated in a small farming community. Roman *smallholders* grew grapes and olives and other Mediterranean crops. They used iron ploughs yoked to oxen. They became soldiers of Rome only when the demands of their farms allowed. As Rome prospered, people became professional soldiers.

Wealthy citizens bought up the small farms to make huge estates that employed hundreds of slaves. They rotated their crops and even understood that planting *legumes* periodically would make their soil more fertile.

A vineyard in ancient Rome.

17

THE MIDDLE AGES

For farmers in Europe, during the Middle Ages, life was hard. Most were *serfs*, peasants who owned no land of their own but were obliged to rent fields from a rich landowner. They worked the noble's fields as well as their own, and had few rights. They grew cereals and vegetables, and kept a few pigs and cattle. Fields were usually divided into strips. Everyone had a share in areas of common land, where cattle could be grazed. One in two, or one in three fields was left to lie fallow. From the little they produced in their own fields, the serfs had to pay to have their grain milled and their bread baked. They also had to do running repairs to the estate.

☐ A hard life

The peasants' own homes were small huts with sacks of straw for beds, and maybe a yard for a few chickens. People ate mostly bread and vegetables, with eggs and chicken occasionally, and any wild creatures such as rabbits and hares that they could catch. Only the nobility could afford much meat, which could be preserved by salting or smoking. Hunting wild animals was reserved for the rich. In England a poor man could be hanged for killing a lord's deer.

☐ Working through the seasons

Winter was the hardest time of all. Fresh food of any kind was scarce and people often went hungry. In spring, the whole community went to work in the fields. Men pushed wooden ploughs pulled by oxen. Women scattered the seed, and children acted as scarecrows to frighten away hungry birds. Children worked as hard as adults. They herded geese to market, and drove pigs into the woods to root for acorns.

Harvest was a busy time for everyone. People prayed for good weather. After the rains that made the crops grow, they needed sunshine to ripen them. Come harvest time, people worked from sunrise to sunset. Grain was taken to the mill to be made into flour. Apples and nuts were picked and stored for winter. Pigs were killed and their meat was made into bacon and ham, ready to be hung up from roof beams, next to bags of dried beans and peas.

☐ Isolation and strife

Farmers in the Middle Ages worked hard to survive, but often whole villages were wiped out by disease or starvation, or by wars fought heedlessly over the land. Farm communities were often isolated, because roads were few and bad. People in one village often treated people in the next village, over the hill, as strangers. For them, it was an adventure to journey to town on market day to sell a cow and buy some trinkets or woollen cloth.

Medieval peasants worked on strips of land owned by a rich lord. They shared the common land, where they could graze cattle and pigs.

19

FARMERS OF THE NEW WORLD

When Europeans first arrived in North and South America they found that the land was farmed. The Indians of the northeast had cultivated a variety of wild plants for thousands of years. They grew corn, beans, squash and many other vegetables. They taught the *settlers* how to grow and cook many foods that were strange to them.

Pioneer families in America had to be practically self-sufficient. Here father is making bullets, mother is making candles, sons and neighbours are tending crops. To survive in the New World, the newcomers had to stick together and help each other.

THE INCAS

When the Spanish arrived in South America in 1532, they found an empire in the Andes that relied on expert farming methods. The army that had conquered the empire had been well fed from storehouses filled by the work of peasant farmers, who grew mostly corn and potatoes, and herded llamas. Only the river valleys were flat and fertile, the rest of the land was mountainous or desert. The farmers skilfully terraced the hillsides and irrigated the fields with canals.

The Incas were rulers of this empire. They owned all the land and dictated how it should be farmed and its produce shared. One third went to feed the priests and provide offerings to the gods. One third went to the emperor's storehouses. From these, food was dispensed to soldiers, nobles, officials and craftsmen, and to those who could not provide for themselves – widows and orphans, the old, the sick and the disabled. The rest of the land went to the peasants. They had to work the land of the gods and the emperor before they tended their own fields.

Llamas provided the Incas with milk, meat, wool and transport.

☐ Clearing the land

Before they could farm their land, the settlers had to clear it. Parties of *pioneers* set out to make new homes in what was to them a strange and frightening wilderness. When they arrived at a good place, the first task for everyone was to rid the area of trees and rocks. They worked with axes and any tools they had brought with them. If they were lucky, established neighbours would lend them a hand. While they cleared the land, they lived in makeshift shelters, with an open fire to warm them and keep wild beasts away.

Until they harvested their first crop, there would be no fresh food to eat, other than animals they could catch in the forest or fish from the streams. Once they had sown their seeds, the pioneers turned their attention to building homes and furnishing them. There was no shortage of wood or craftsmen skilled in woodworking. Families worked together to raise the timbers.

NATIVE FARMERS OF THE AMERICAS

Forest Indians in the north hunted deer for their meat and for their hides. Some communities lived in *wigwams* made of hides. Some lived in *longhouses*, shared by several families.

On the plains, some Indians would plant crops in the spring, hunt buffalo (bison) during the summer, and return to their fields for the harvest. During the summer they lived in *tepees* made of buffalo hide.

The Indians of the southwest were crop-growers who irrigated their fields. They lived together in high terraced homes made of adobe (sun-baked clay).

In the Caribbean the people built thatched homes in villages. They grew beans, cassava, potatoes and corn, and picked the luscious fruits that grew wild.

☐ Days of toil

Once settled, the pioneers still had to battle to keep the wilderness at bay and protect themselves from hostile Indians whose land they had taken. The settlers built stockades around their villages, and nobody ventured out without a rifle at the ready.

Men, women and children shared all the farmwork and all the housework. There was plenty of it. There were few shops to buy goods in, so almost everything had to be home-made. Women would make cheese one day, clothes the next, candles and ammunition the next.

Children would grind corn in the morning and maybe have lessons in the afternoons. The days were rarely long enough to get all the jobs done.

☐ Slaves from Africa

Cotton, tobacco, sugar cane and other crops were grown on plantations in North America and the West Indies. Most of the plantations were established by British settlers. The workers on the plantations were slaves brought from Africa from the 1640s onwards. The produce was mostly shipped back to Europe. Until the mid-1800s slaves could be bought and sold by their white masters. Some owners treated their slaves fairly, but most were forced to work long hours in gangs and in return received just enough food to keep their strength up. Others were treated even more cruelly. The slaves preserved memories of their African homeland in music and stories, and these have become part of black culture in America today.

In the forests of South America, the Indians cleared patches of land on which to grow cassava, potatoes, peppers, corn and manioc – a root vegetable like cassava. They lived in open-sided houses with a thatch of palm leaves. In some places the villagers built one big house for everyone.

The longhorn cattle of the American West were wily, wild animals. Rounding them up was a lot more dangerous than driving a herd of docile modern cattle.

HOME ON THE RANGE

Cattle were brought to the New World by the Spanish in the 1500s. By the mid-1800s ranchers in the southwest were raising cattle on the open *range* – vast stretches of unfenced land. Cowboys were hired to brand the animals, round them up, and drive them across the range. They lived in the saddle by day and camped by a fire at night. It was a hard, dangerous and comfortless life.

Later *ranches* were fenced in. Cowboys lived together in *bunkhouses*, but their lives grew no less dangerous. They still had to cope with often cruel weather, cattle *stampedes* and disputes with neighbours. At night the cowboys sang songs and told stories, or rode into town. There was not much time or opportunity for family life.

> **SHAPING THE LAND**
>
> Farmers have made the countryside we see around us. The great prairies of North America have been ploughed for cereal crops. The forests of Europe have been cleared for fields and vineyards. The hillsides of Southeast Asia have been carefully *terraced* for rice cultivation. Every farming community shapes the land and is shaped by it.

TOWARDS TODAY

From the 1500s, richer farmers in Europe began to 'enclose' their fields. They bought land from neighbours, and hedged or fenced it to keep out other farmers' animals. This change made farms more efficient, but it affected the life of the farm community. Many poor people once again became farm labourers, working for a rich farmer. They no longer owned their own plots of land. Often they lived in small houses owned by the farmer, and were unable to move away. Some farm workers in Europe live in *tied cottages* to this day.

Improvements in farming methods continued. New tools and machines were invented, and new industries grew up to process, package and market food. The farmer's wife no longer had to make the cheese, it could be done by machine. Cattle were slaughtered and their meat packed far from the farms where they were reared.

☐ **Traditional farms disappear**

By the 1900s, farms had changed even more. Some farms were now very large. Others were run by *tenants*, renting the land from a landowner. Some farms were run by farm managers, employed by agricultural companies. Machines took over much of the farmwork that had formerly been done by people. *Combine harvesters* replaced gangs of workers with *scythes* and *sickles*. Electric milking machines replaced milkmaids, and tractors replaced horses. Traditional mixed farms were becoming rarer but some still exist today.

A tranquil country scene. This is how townsfolk like to imagine the countryside: peaceful, traditional and unchanging. Many farms are now large businesses, but there are still plenty of small family-run farms that raise cows, pigs, poultry and perhaps sheep, as well as growing root, grain and other crops.

Farming Today

In temperate lands where soils are fertile and there is plenty of rain, relatively few people work in farming. Traditional mixed farms that once provided a balanced diet for the local community have given place to specialized farms whose produce may be sold to people thousands of miles away. Large areas of farmland have no farm animals, and large areas no crops. In poor countries, more people work on the land but produce less than farmers in rich countries.

Large areas of the world are too cold, too dry, too mountainous or too built up for agricultural production. These areas are less developed as a result. Third World yields could be improved, however, if the countries could afford more modern farming methods.

Rich farm land	Forest	Cereal crops	Livestock
Poor farm land	Desert	Fruit	

PRAIRIE GRAIN GROWERS

On the vast treeless prairies of the United States and Canada, farmers grow millions of tonnes of grain each year. Much is exported to countries that cannot feed their own people.

The farmers live in small and often lonely communities. From the air, the prairies look like a vast sea of wheat, with clusters of farm buildings scattered here and there like islands. These enormous farms need surprisingly few people to work them, because most of the work has been *mechanized*. Tractors haul the ploughs and seed-drills, and at harvest time armies of combine harvesters march across the fields. The grain is stored in tall *elevators* that are often the only landmarks.

NEW WHEAT

Living in the prairie communities are many people whose ancestors were pioneer settlers. The Mennonites, for example, were a religious group who came to the United States from Russia in the 1870s. They introduced a variety of wheat, called Turkey Red, which grew well on the dry plains. This new wheat made possible the great expansion of wheat farming, especially in Kansas and other US states.

New strains of wheat that will ripen quickly have produced increased yields all over the world. In places where the hours of daylight were too few to ripen old varieties, the new varieties grow with vigour.

☐ From village to town

As farms have grown larger and transport has become easier, traditional farming communities have virtually disappeared. The village community has become a town community. There is no call for little local stores when people can buy all they need in a shopping mall and store a year's supply of food in their freezer. There is no need for a village school when children can take the bus to town. In many villages public transport is becoming a thing of the past, leaving the old and poor isolated.

The town supplies all the community's needs. It has churches and schools, doctors, hospitals and vets, shops and car showrooms, banks and all kinds of businesses. Farmers can buy new machinery and equipment and sell their produce at the auction barns and grain elevators.

The North American prairies are a sea of wheat. Farmers use fertilizers to improve the soil, herbicides to control weeds, pesticides to prevent disease, and more machines than people to plough, plant and gather the grain.

DEPRESSION AND DUST

Old people still remember the hard times in the 1930s, when farm prices fell during the worldwide economic depression. On the American plains, the rains also failed, and terrible dust storms blew away the dry topsoil. Many farmers gave up when their fields were turned to dust. Those who stayed have tried to stop soil erosion. But fears of a second Dust Bowl disaster remain.

Farmers no longer call on their neighbours for help with the harvest. They hire workers and pay them the going rate for the job. They no longer rely on the Saturday-night barn dance for their entertainment. They can go to restaurants and clubs, or stay at home and watch the television.

☐ **Keeping up with each other**

In most county towns government farm agencies are available to help and advise farmers. Research into crops and farming methods brings constant improvements, so farmers make sure that they are up to date with the latest techniques and products. Although farmers compete with each other, they keep in contact and discuss problems and pass on information to each other.

HOME ON THE RANGE

In Australia, the United States and South America farmers rear cattle and sheep in huge numbers on enormous open ranges of grassland. These people are used to looking after themselves, for the nearest neighbour may be miles away. Some ranches are so big that the farmers use helicopters to get about.

☐ Modern cowboys

Once cowboys spent almost the whole working day in the saddle. Horses are still used on many ranches, but modern cowboys mostly use motorbikes or trucks. They use radios to keep in touch with the ranch boss, with their fellow workers and with their homes.

Ranching is big business today. Huge herds of finely bred cattle are raised on lush pasture to ensure that the American public gets only the most succulent, tender beef in its hamburgers and steaks. The cattle are fed and housed in dry sheds when the weather is bad.

Though the cattle are more docile than the longhorns of old, dealing with so many animals demands strength and courage. A cowboy no longer needs a gun to fight off hostile Indians or cattle *rustlers*, but the modern cowboy still faces dangers. Snow in winter can bury cattle. Drought in summer parches the land, dries up water holes and withers pasture. Storms can turn gentle streams into tumbling torrents. But life at home is a lot more comfortable.

☐ **Family life**

Ranch families have cars, televisions, deep freezes and other modern conveniences, and they are no longer isolated. They can drive into town to shop and visit friends. Children take the bus to school. They eat the same fast food and watch the same television shows as everyone else. Though most ranch children learn to ride and occasionally see a visiting rodeo show, rodeo riders on bucking broncos are more familiar to them in movies than in real life.

Above: The gauchos are the cowboys of South America. Riding across the pampas, or grasslands, they herd the beef cattle for which Argentina is famous.

Opposite: Cattle are pampered to produce fine beef. They eat ten times more food than they produce. In less developed countries meat is a luxury few people can afford.

Right: The busy stockyards of Oklahoma deal with millions of cattle raised on the ranches of this important US beef-producing state.

The heart of Australia is desert. Vast sheep stations in the outback produce enough pasture for sheep on land that would be too dry to grow crops. Motorcycles are often used to round up the sheep.

FARMERS OF AUSTRALASIA

Many farms remain family businesses, in which family members share the work. A dairy farm in New Zealand, for example, might have 130 cows. Only two people are needed to look after the cattle. So father and one son can manage it. Instead of riding horses or walking, they ride around on motorbikes. Other children must find work in the town.

Milk from cows is made into *dairy foods* such as butter and cheese. Often farmers organize *co-operatives* to make and sell these dairy foods.

☐ Faraway farmers

Farming can be a lonely life. Farmers may spend a day on the farm without seeing anyone. So they look forward to the next trip to town, for a chat with neighbours about farm prices, and to catch up with the local news. Dairy farmers know that if they go to bed late, they still have to

Teams of sheep shearers travel from station to station. With so many millions of sheep to be sheared, the shearers take pride in the speed with which they can cut away the fleeces without harming the sheep.

The doctor comes by air in isolated parts of Australia.

Lessons come over the air for these Australian children who live hundreds of miles from the nearest school.

be up early for the morning milking. Children have to be up early, too, to make the long bus journey to school. Their mothers may only get to town every few months. Many farms are so isolated that people have to travel to town by plane.

Many children receive their education without ever moving from their homes. They do their lessons by radio. When people are sick the doctor may fly in to visit them. If they are very ill, they are air-lifted to hospital.

☐ **Alone with hundreds of sheep**
The loneliest life is that of the hill shepherd. He or she has a dog and a flock of sheep for company. In Australia, huge flocks of sheep are kept on ranches called sheep stations. Once a year, at *shearing* time, a contractor's shearing gang arrives. The shearers go from station to station, working at great speed. They are proud of their skill, and take part in hotly contested competitions to see who is the fastest and best shearer.

SURVIVING IN ASIA

Farmers in rich countries often complain. They complain about high taxes and low prices; about the expense of buying new tractors, fuel for heating, fertilizers, and animal feed. A poor peasant farmer in an overcrowded country like Bangladesh in Asia faces even more serious problems.

Bangladesh is a flat land, with many rivers. It is a desperately poor country, with few natural resources. Yet it is home to more than 104 million people. Farmers in Bangladesh struggle to grow food for themselves. Their greatest enemy is flooding, because the land is so low-lying and open to the sea. Farmers plant their crops on fields raised on mud banks, for protection against floodwaters.

Few farmers in Bangladesh have money to buy tractors or fertilizers. The people build their own houses. Women work as hard as men, helping to till the

This Indian woman has to carry home huge bundles of leaves to burn as fuel for cooking the family meal.

Bangladeshi farmers in a rice field. Bangladesh is very flat and low-lying. Mud banks offer little protection to crops or homes when cyclones strike, and terrible floods occur.

soil with wooden hand-ploughs. There is endless work, and almost no leisure.

☐ Families at work

In the West, there are now fewer family farms. But family farming is still common in Asia. In India the oldest man in the family owns the land. Three or four generations share a home. Young men do not move away when they marry. When a girl marries, she goes to live with her husband's family. She brings an extra pair of hands to help with the work, but also an extra mouth to feed.

On a peasant farm in Asia or Africa women often do the heavy work. They carry water from the well, *manure* the fields with cattle dung, and gather firewood for cooking. In semi-desert lands, where trees are scarce, collecting firewood may take hours every day. Some farmers burn cow dung on their cooking fires, and so waste a valuable natural fertilizer.

CYCLONE PERIL

From time to time, terrible tropical storms called cyclones rush in from the Bay of Bengal. The winds drive the sea inland. Water pours over the farmers' fields, villages are swamped, houses swept away, cattle drowned. Many people lose their few precious possessions. In the worst floods, thousands of people die.

Despite these natural disasters, the farmers of Bangladesh do not give up. Each new season brings new hope. Even after a cyclone, people return to their land as soon as the waters have fallen. They rebuild their homes, plough the salt-soaked soil, and plant new seeds for a new harvest. Aid from richer countries is some help, but the villagers themselves must do most of the work to reclaim the drowned land.

PLANTATIONS

The tea in your tea bag may have come from the leaves of a bush growing on a hillside in India or Sri Lanka. Women pick the leaves from the plants by hand, and drop them into baskets hung on their backs. The leaves are taken to the tea estate factory, where other workers watch over the rolling machines, fermentation tables, and driers that turn the fresh green leaves into dark fragments ready for packing.

Most plantations are owned by large international companies. They are factory farms, employing large numbers of workers. Much of the work, picking the leaves from tea bushes for example, is done by women. They work hard, often for low wages.

Some plantation workers live in houses built by the company. Often in the past such workers were not much better off than slaves. Because they were forced to buy goods from company-owned stores, workers often got into debt. They ended up working just to repay the company who employed them.

PEASANT FARMERS OF THE ANDES

In the high Andes mountains of South America, peasant farmers till the soil much as their ancestors did hundreds of years ago. Some farmers still use *digging sticks* instead of spades, and oxen instead of tractors. It is bitterly cold in the thin air of the bleak highlands, and few crops grow well. Often the people go hungry.

☐ **Wage slaves**

In the past, the Indians of the Andes were treated as slaves by the Spanish conquerors. Today, they have regained some of their lost lands, though most of the best land is owned by wealthy families. The landowners employ workers on low wages to plant and harvest profitable crops. Where government land reforms have given land back to the people, they still have problems. Many people are too poor to buy seed, let alone fertilizers or the machines and equipment they need to irrigate and run their farms.

FESTIVALS

The traditional Inca festivals were linked to the farming year. There was a Mother Earth festival for ploughing time, a festival of the storm god to bring rain to new crops, and a great sun festival to celebrate the harvest.

These ancient rituals are now woven into the calendar of the Catholic Church. Catholic priests brought Christianity to the Aymara and Quechua Indians of Ecuador, Peru and Bolivia in the 1500s.

Today when the Indians parade through the streets, are they celebrating their ancient sun god as well as the feast of Corpus Christi, which falls at the same time?

Farming in Peru, in the foothills of the Andes Mountains. Oxen are used to plough the valley soil, but there is much backbreaking work for the peasants, often with little reward.

Others manage to produce enough to feed the family and travel to market in town to sell potatoes, beans, corn and herbs. They accept cash, instead of bartering goods as they once did. Some can afford to buy a radio or television, or even a secondhand motorbike or truck. Some Indian children do not stay in the mountain villages, but drift to the towns and cities, looking for jobs. They often land up jobless and homeless, living in squalid shanty towns. Many resort to crime.

SUBSISTENCE IN AFRICA

In West Africa a farm family hopes to grow all the vegetables it needs. The people plant yams, maize, cassava, okra and peppers, as well as bananas and oil palm trees. Children go to school on weekdays, often walking a long distance through the forest to get there. At weekends they help their parents. The busiest time is the rainy season, from March to September, when weeds spring up all over the vegetable plots. Everyone gets to work with hoes and machetes (long broad-bladed knives).

The children may enjoy their work on the farm, but many see their future in the city. There they may have an opportunity to go to college and study for careers in medicine, law and business. Others may work in

Right: This farmer in Ghana has a fine crop of yams. They are probably his only crop, which he will sell to feed his family, and buy other goods.

Below: A Masai cattle-herder. These East African people are nomads, moving with their herds to find fresh grazing.

Above: In Africa women often look after the children and the family vegetable plot, while the men are away hunting, tilling the fields or, these days, finding work in mines or factories.

factories or drive a truck for a living. As more young people drift away, villages die. Only older people remain, and they cannot keep the land cultivated.

☐ Old ways die

When the old system of subsistence farming breaks down, families can no longer grow enough food to feed themselves. The government has to buy food from abroad. This imported food must be paid for from cash crops, grown on large plantations where workers are paid wages for their labour. Governments in parts of Africa have concentrated on new factories and big plantations where they use modern farming methods and equipment. They have neglected the small farmers, who once grew all the food the people needed.

CATTLE HERDERS OF AFRICA

In parts of Africa people look upon cattle as wealth. A farmer with many cows is rich, no matter how little milk or meat they provide. The Masai people of East Africa are famous as cattle-herders and lion-hunters. The cattle are herded into the village at night, protected by a thornbush fence from attack by hungry lions. A traditional Masai village house is made of mud and dried cow dung. Women live in one room, men in another. The remaining room is shared by children and calves.

☐ The seasonal round

Village farmers move to and from their fields as the seasons change. In Botswana, in southern Africa, people leave their villages to plant the seeds in the fields in spring, after the rainy season. School ends so that older children can help. Only old people and little children are left at home.

Boys help to drive the cattle out to graze on the new grass. As the crops ripen in the hot season, streams run dry and the grass withers. Then the cattle must be brought back to the village, where they can be given drinking water from the well. The villagers return to the fields to bring in the harvest of grain. Village life resumes until the rains come again. People spend the rainy season at home, mending their tools ready for the next planting.

37

NOMADIC HERDERS

Nomads are people who have no fixed homes, but wander with their herds to find fresh grass for the animals to eat. Some nomads keep camels or goats, others drive flocks of sheep. Their animals provide them with milk, meat and clothing.

□ **Living on the steppes**

The herding peoples of eastern Russia and Mongolia are expert horseriders. Their traditional homes are tents, called yurts, made from animal skins. Small boys are given the job of looking after the cattle and sheep. But the horses are half-wild, and it takes experienced riders to round them up. The animals are vital to the nomads' lives. A nomad family will often bring lambs and goat kids into their tent at night for extra warmth.

On the vast treeless steppes of Central Asia a family may travel 100 kilometres to visit relatives. Normally members of the family meet only in the evening for the

Opposite: Today, though few Lapps still wander with their reindeer, they keep up traditional appearances. Their brightly coloured clothes contrast sharply with the bleakness of their lands.

Right: The Bedouin of North Africa and the Middle East are desert people. Camel-herders are aristocrats. Lower in the social scale are sheep and goat herders.

main meal of the day. During the day, the men and boys make do with a snack of cheese soaked in tea. The tea is made from Chinese tea-bricks, brewed in water with salt, flour, butter and milk.

☐ Change comes to the nomads

The Lapp people of Scandinavia live north of the Arctic Circle. Here the sun does not shine for two months of the year, and winter lasts for nine months. It is so bitterly cold that few plants grow. Until valuable metals were found there, the snow-covered land provided only one vital resource – reindeer.

For hundreds of years the Lapps roamed with their reindeer herds, dependent on the animals for all their needs, including transport. It was impossible for them to settle in one place because the vegetation was so sparse. They built huts of turf or wood in the forests and pitched tents made of hide in the open. Today, most Lapps have settled down to town life. They work as foresters or fishermen or on farms. Some even work in the mines.

Above: In Mongolia, children learn to ride a horse as soon as (or before) they can walk. Keeping a watchful eye on the camels is more fun when you have a pony for a companion.

MIGRANT WORKERS

Some farm workers in developed countries move from place to place to find work. They move to an area as fruit or vegetable crops grow ripe. They pick them for low wages and live in temporary accommodation, often with poor sanitary facilities. These people generally live in poverty because their work is seasonal and underpaid, and they do not stay in one place long enough to receive government health and other benefits to which they are entitled.

COMMUNES AND COLLECTIVES

In most countries farmers own their own land. Sons and daughters may help with work on the farm, and the same piece of land may stay in one family for hundreds of years. But sometimes the family sells the land to another farmer or to somebody who wants to build houses or factories on it. In some countries the land is taken from rich landowners by the government.

☐ **Collective farms**

In the 1930s the communist government in Russia took land away from farmers and forced people to work on big state-run farms. This *collective* farming did not work very well because most people were happier looking after their own small plots of land. Other communist countries tried similar plans, but most have had to return to a

---

CO-OPERATION AND CORPORATE FARMS

Farmers in the West often join together in voluntary co-operatives. Five dairy farmers in one area might get a better price for their milk if they sell it together. Grain farmers often band together to build an elevator where all their wheat can be stored and sold. People have more of an incentive to work hard on land of their own that they can pass on to a son or daughter, but often that is not the most efficient way to farm. Some family farms have grown into large businesses and are run as *corporate farms*.

China has more people, and more farmers, than any other country. During the upheavals of the 'cultural revolution' in the 1960s, many townspeople were moved to the country to work on communal farms (below left). In remote provinces like Sinkiang, in northwest China, luxuries are in short supply. In this settlement (below, right), horse riders outnumber trucks.

system that allows small farmers more freedom to look after their own land.

In China some farmworkers also have jobs in factories. Women work in the fields by day, and at night try to make a bit more money by making clothes for sale. Often grandparents, parents and children live together in one farmhouse. They keep pigs, sheep and cattle, and grow rice, vegetables and herbs. Farmers in northern China grow wheat, because the climate is too cold for rice. But in the warm south, rice and other crops can be grown all year round.

☐ **A plot of one's own**

A Chinese farm family lives simply. For many, home is a house made from mud bricks. Inside there may be a few modern conveniences, now that electricity has reached most Chinese villages. People listen to the radio, and a few lucky families own a television. Almost everyone rides a bicycle. Some people own motorbikes, but very few people can afford a car or truck. People walk miles along the dusty roads, carrying farm produce on their backs to sell in the market.

Some Chinese farmers still live in *communes*. These government-run farms are like small towns, with their own schools, hospitals and nurseries for babies. Everyone joins in the work in the communal fields, but each family also has a private plot, and can choose what crops to grow and sell.

41

☐ Life on a kibbutz

In Israel, many farm families live on *kibbutzim*. These are communal farms, where people share everything. The kibbutz owns all property. The people make their own rules, and vote on matters that affect the community. Everyone has a job. In return for their work, everyone receives food, shelter, schooling and medical care. Young children spend their day in the nursery in the children's house, while their parents are at work. They hardly see their parents during the day. But families meet to talk and relax in the communal dining room. Here the day starts early with breakfast together, and ends with supper when the day's work is over.

Much of Israel is desert, land that is too dry to be farmed. The first kibbutz was set up in 1909. In 1948 the state of Israel was founded. Thousands of Jews from Europe and elsewhere came to live there. They needed food. With the help of grants and loans from abroad, the people set about *reclaiming* the desert by skilful irrigation. They now grow numerous crops and export fruit and vegetables to countries all round the world.

The kibbutz settlements succeed because the people who live in them share a common purpose. People are ready to give up some privacy and individual freedom because they see benefits in working together. They live as pioneers in a new country, overcoming many dangers and difficulties.

Above: People on a kibbutz in Israel picking grapefruit. Working together is part of kibbutz life.

Left: A kibbutz community is like an extended family. The children learn, play and eat as a group while their parents are working.

THREAT OF WAR

The Israelis have made the desert green, but for many years their land has known no peace because of Israel's quarrel with its Arab neighbours. Many kibbutzim are within range of hostile forces. They have fortifications and are guarded night and day.

Farming in the Modern World

Farmers often look back to the past, when the farmer was a pioneer who cleared the land, tilled the virgin soil, and turned wilderness into fruitful fields. Farm life was at the heart of every nation. Farming in the future will be very different.

Natural disasters usually hit the poorest hardest. Locusts are the scourge of African farmers. One swarm of these insects can destroy a year's crop in minutes.

In the past, almost all farms were family-sized and family-run. In poor countries, most farms are still small. Governments and aid organizations encourage farmers to work together in communes. A peasant owning a tiny plot of land cannot produce food efficiently. A group of neighbours forming a commune can afford to buy better seed, fertilizers and farm tools. The commune can afford to hire a tractor, and pay the vet to treat sick animals. Everyone benefits. The farmers decide together how the farm will be run, and share out the proceeds.

☐ **Green revolution**
The world's farmers produce more food than ever before. Scientists have brought about a green revolution, through the use of improved fertilizers and pesticides, and advances in crop and animal breeding. These advances have helped feed the world's hungry millions. Yet in famine-stricken countries, such as Ethiopia, people still die of starvation. The Earth's human population is growing at an alarming rate while the amount of land available for farming is unlikely to increase. Can we grow enough food to feed 10 billion people in the next century? No one can be sure.

☐ **Farming tomorrow**
Today, there are fewer farms and fewer farmers. In the 1930s there were more than six million farms in the

Drought and civil war have brought famine to parts of Africa. These hungry people in Ethiopia wait patiently for food brought by relief workers.

43

United States. Now there are only two million. In 1900 the average size of an American farm was 59 hectares. Now it is three times as big: 184 hectares. Many farms have become more like factories.

Farms today have fewer farmworkers. In the 1800s one farmworker was needed to grow enough food for four people. Now, that same worker could produce enough food for 80 people.

☐ From farms to factories

Some farming communities have gone for ever. The Santa Clara Valley, near San Francisco in California, was once a rich *orchard* region, with farms producing plums, pears, apricots, cherries and other fruits. The orchards have now gone, and in their place are computer factories. Orchard Valley has become Silicon Valley, a busy industrial and business region.

☐ Changing tastes

The modern farmer must heed the demands of stores and of customers. If shoppers want more chicken, and less beef, then the beef farmer may find his income dwindling, and may have to change to chicken rearing.

GREEN WORLD

Only a few of the world's natural *habitats* remain. Most of the forests and grasslands have been turned into farmland. Over-use of the land and pollution from fertilizers and pesticides have created many environmental problems that must be solved before more damage is done. The world's tropical forests are now under threat. Many trees are being cut down for timber. Huge areas of forest have already been destroyed.

Forest communities in Asia and South America have tried to stop the destruction of the forests on which they depend. But they are powerless against the logging companies, with their bulldozers and chainsaws. If the world is to remain green and healthy, international measures must be taken to stop more natural habitats being despoiled.

Opposite: Once this land in Israel was desert. Now, thanks to soil irrigation and good soil management, olive trees thrive.

Above: Science can make barren soil bloom. Alaska has a harsh climate. But with modern seeds and techniques, barley can now be grown there. With improved varieties and better control of the environment, many more unproductive areas could be cultivated to feed the world's poor.

Farmers in less-developed countries, who grow single crops such as cocoa or coffee, are hit if prices drop because people eat less chocolate or decide that drinking too much coffee is bad for their health.

Some farmers have to sell their land, to make room for housing, or factories, or a new road. Where there is over-production of a particular crop, governments encourage farmers to use their land in other ways. Some have made their farms into holiday homes or golf courses, or parks where townspeople can come to enjoy country life and see farm animals. The farmer may make more money from tourism than from farming.

☐ **Facing the challenge**

In most countries the traditional picture-book farm, with its farmyard and mixture of animals, has vanished. The modern farmer is more likely to sit at a computer than to drive a horse and wagon. But farmers are still tied to their land. Their lives are governed by the rhythm of the seasons. Farmers everywhere face the same challenge. They must work in harmony with nature to produce our food, but also to protect the environment, and the plants and animals that share our world.

Glossary

Auction Public sale in which crops, animals or other articles are sold to the highest bidder.
Bartering Exchanging produce or goods for someone else's produce or goods.
Battery hens are reared and fattened in sheds for their eggs or meat.
Breed A particular kind of animal or plant. Farmers breed animals and plants by helping them produce offspring. They produce new varieties by breeding different types with different qualities.
Bunkhouses Simple buildings providing sleeping quarters for cowboys and other workers. With several beds to a room, the cowboys 'bunked up' together.
Cash crops are grown for sale, rather than to be eaten by the farmer's family.
Cereal crops are food plants such as wheat, rice, barley, oats, millet and sorghum.
Collective farms are formed from several small holdings. Voluntary collectives have produced efficient results in some countries, but state-controlled collectives in communist countries have usually been less successful.
Combine harvester Machine which cuts wheat (and other cereals), and separates the grain from the stalks, ready for storing.
Commune Community where people share everything and decide together how to run their affairs.
Co-operative Arrangement by which farmers run their own farms, but work together to sell their produce.
Corporate farm Farm owned and run by a large business or corporation. Some corporate farms are family farms.
Crop rotation Planting a different crop in a plot of land each season. Rotation prevents the build-up of plant disease in the soil.
Dairy foods Foods, such as butter, cheese and yogurt, which are made from milk, and eggs from chickens.
Digging sticks Wooden implements used for turning the soil that farmers used before metal tools were invented. Digging sticks are still used in some countries.
Domesticate To make animals tame enough to rear and breed for food and other uses.
Drought Period without rainfall.
Elevator A grain elevator is a tall building, usually made of steel, that is used to store grain.
Factory farms On factory farms animals, such as calves or chickens, are not allowed to range freely. They are kept and fed in temperature-controlled sheds.
Fallow land Farmland that is allowed to rest for a year or season without a crop, to regain its fertility.
Famines occur when food supplies become extremely scarce and people starve to death. They may be caused by severe drought, crop failure, war and over-population.
Fertilizer A natural or artificial chemical substance that is added to soil to make it more fertile.
Food processing is necessary to prevent food going bad and to present it in a form that pleases the customer.
Germinate A seed germinates when it puts down a root and sends up its first shoot. Seeds need water to germinate.
Gluts occur when the supply of a crop or product exceeds the demand for it.
Grain Seeds from wheat and other cereal plants that contain nutritious starch, protein and oil.
Habitat Natural home of a plant or animal, or a collection of them.
Harvest Time for gathering in ripe crops.
Herbicides Chemicals used to kill plants. Most are selective, killing weeds while leaving crops undamaged.
Intensive farming methods are used to get as high a yield as possible from farmland or farm animals.
Irrigation Watering crops by artificial means, for example, by digging canals and ditches to carry water from a river.
Kibbutzim Farm communities in Israel, where people live and work together, sharing everything.
Latex Liquid that oozes from a rubber tree, and is used to make rubber.
Legumes are members of the pea family. They produce their seeds in pods and their roots fix nitrogen in the soil and make it more fertile.
Livestock Animals that are raised on farms for use or sale.
Longhouses Communal houses in which many primitive families share accommodation.
Manure Natural fertilizer, such as green plants or animal dung.
Market Place where goods are bought and sold. Farmers in many countries carry their own produce, or drive their animals, to market in the nearest town.
Mechanize To use machines to do jobs that were formerly done by people.
Mixed farm A farm where crops are grown and animals are reared.

An arable farm grows only crops. Other farms such as pig farms, ranches or sheep stations keep only animals.
Monsoon Wind that brings the wet and dry seasons to south and east Asia.
Nomads People who wander about with their herds of grazing animals, such as sheep, cattle or camels.
Orchard Plantation of fruit trees, such as apples, pears or plums.
Peasant A farmer who owns a small plot of land.
Perishable foods are those that do not keep for long and have to be preserved in some way.
Pesticides Chemicals used to kill insect pests.
Pharaoh King in ancient Egypt.
Pioneers Original settlers who make the way ready for others.
Plantations Large farms planted with a single crop, such as cotton, tea or bananas.
Plough To dig the soil, by turning it with the blade of a plough, to prepare it for planting.
Pollution The dirtying of the environment with poisonous or unpleasant substances.
Prairies Flat or rolling, treeless plains that were naturally grass-covered and are now used for growing wheat.
Produce Food or other products from a farm or plantation.
Ranches Very large farms where cattle or other animals are reared. In Australia they are called stations.
Range Large, open stretch of grazing land.
Reclaiming Bringing land back into use that was formerly unusable, such as desert or land that was flooded.
Retailers sell goods in small quantities to the public. Wholesalers sell in larger quantities to retailers. Producers, such as farmers, sell in bulk to wholesalers.
Rustlers Cattle thieves, so-called because of the tell-tale soft rustling sound they make as they commit their crimes.
Scythes Tools with long curved blades and long wooden handles, used by farmworkers to cut crops.
Seasons Times of the year with distinct climates. In temperate regions, the four seasons are winter, spring, summer and autumn, or fall.
Serfs People who worked on the land and were partly slaves. Serfdom was widespread during the Middle Ages and persisted in Russia until this century.
Settlers People who move to live in a new area. America is peopled by the descendants of settlers from all over the world.
Shaduf Device used for irrigating fields in ancient Egypt. It consists of a bucket on the end of a long pole and can be worked by people or tethered animals.
Shearing Cutting away the wool, or fleece, of sheep.
Sickles Tools with short handles and semi-circular blades, used by farmworkers to cut crops.
Smallholders Owners of small areas of agricultural land. A smallholding is smaller than a farm.
Stampedes Sudden scatterings of cattle or other animals panicking in fright.
Steppes European equivalent of the prairies.
Subsistence farmers grow just enough to feed one family, or village, with nothing left over for sale.
Temperate zones have a moderate climate with four seasons. They lie between the tropics and the polar regions.
Tenants have temporary ownership of land or dwellings.
Tepees Conical Indian tents made of skins stretched over a frame of converging poles.
Terraced hillsides have a series of level areas cut into them, like steps. They retain enough soil and moisture for farmers to grow crops that could never grow on the natural slopes.
Third World Term used to describe the poor and under-developed nations of the world. Most Third World countries are in Africa and Asia.
Tied cottages are homes for farmworkers that go with the job. If the farmworker loses his job, he loses his home, too.
Wholesalers buy goods and produce from producers to sell to retailers.
Wigwams Indian huts.
Yield The amount of a crop or crops that a piece of land produces.

47

Index

Agricultural shows and fairs 14-15, *14*
Auction 14, 46

Barbecues 15
Barn dances 15, *15*
Bartering 16, 46
Battery hens 46
Beer 16
Breed, breeding 43, 46
Bunkhouses 23, 46

Cash crops 10, *14*, 37, 46
Cash crops: effect of demand on 45
Cattle 7, 10, 16, 18, 28-29, *29*
　longhorn 23
　showing *14*
Cattle herding 37, *36*
Cereals 10, 18, *25*, 46
Children's work 18, 22-23, 29, 31, *31*, 36, 37, 38, *39*
Coffee, tea and cocoa 11, 34, *34*, 45
Collective farms 40-41, 46
Combine harvester 24, 46
Common land 18, *19*
Commune, communal farms 41, *41*, 46
　modernizing 43
Co-operatives 40, 46
Corn goddess 13, *13*
Corporate farms 40, 46
Cow dung 33
Cowboys 23, *23*, 28-29 *29*
Crop diseases 10
Crop failure 9
Crop rotation 11, 17, 46
Crops 10-11, 16, *22*
　collectives 41
　subsistence 36, *36*
Cyclone peril 33

Dairy farming, foods 30-31, 46
Digging sticks 34, 46
Domestication 7, 46
Drought 9, 10, 12, 29, 46
Dust Bowl 26

Elevators 26, 46
Extensive farming 10

Factory farms *7*, 8, 46
Fallow land 11, 46
Famine 9, 12, 43, *43*, 46
Farm agencies 27
Farm labourers 24, 27, 39
　leaving the land 8
　wages 9
Farm managers 24
Farm sizes 8
Farmer's year 12-13
　subsistence farming 37
Farming: kinds of 10-11
　modern *7*, 8-9
Farming communities 7, 8-9, 20, *22-23*, 2
　decline of 26, 44
　isolation 19
Farming festivals 35
Farming methods: improvements in 24
　modern 37
Farms: decline in numbers 43-44
　enlarging 17, 24, 43
Fertilizer 9, 32, 43, 44, 46
　pollution from 9, 44
Fibre 11
Fields: division of 18
　'enclosure' of 24
Firewood collecting 33, *32*
Flooding 16, 17, 32, *32*, 33
Flying doctor *31*

Food: price paid for 9
　taxes on 17
Food processing and packaging 9, 12, 18, 24, 46
Forest: clearance of 20, 24
　stopping destruction of 44
Fruit growing 10, 11, 16, *16*, 17, *25*
　harvesting 18

Gauchos 29
Germination 46
Gluts 10, 46
Goats 7, 11, 16
Grain, grain growing 16, 17, 26-27, *26*, 46
　effect of improving 45
　grinding 18
　harvesting 12
　marketing 14
Green revolution 43
Green world 44

Habitat 46
Haggling (bargaining) 14
Harvest 12-13, *12*, 18, 26, 46
　failure of 10, 12
Harvest festival and suppers 7, 9, 13
Harvest moon 13
Herbicides 46
Horses 15, *39*, *41*
Housing 21, *20*, 22, *22*, 24, 32, 34, 37, 38, 41
Hunting 18

Incas 20, *20*
Insect pests 10, 12
Intensive farming 8, 10, 46
Irrigation 9, 16, *16*, 17, *22*, 42, *45*, 46

Kibbutz, kibbutzim 42, *42*, 46

Latex 46
Legumes 46
　and fertility 17
Leisure industry 45
Livestock, livestock farming 7, 10-11, 16, 17, 38-39, *39*, 41, 46
　effects of demand on 44-45
　selling 9, 10, 14
Llamas 20, *20*
Locusts 12
Longhouses *22*, 46

Manure 33, 46
Market 12, 46
　getting produce to 9, 12, 19, 41
Masai 37, *36*
Mechanization 26, 28, 30, *30*, 43, 46
Migrant workers 39
Milking machines, electric 24
Mixed farming 11, *24*, 46
　decline of 24
Monsoon 12, 47

Nile, River 16
Nomads *36*, 38-39, *39*, 47
Nuts 11
　harvesting 18

Oilseeds 11
Orchards 47
　disappearance of 44
Overseas aid 33
Over-use of land 44

Peasant farmers 10, 18, *19*, 34-35, *35*, 47
　Third World 32-33, *32*
Perishable goods 12, 47
Pesticides 9, 43, 44, 47
　pollution from 9, 44
Pharaoh 17, 47
Pigs 7, 11, 16, 18
　processing 18
Pineapple harvest 13
Pioneers 20-23, *20*, 47

Plantations 11, 23, 34, *34*, 37, 47
Ploughing, for prizes 15
Ploughs 47
　iron 17
　mechanized 26
　pulled by oxen 16
　wooden 10, 18, 33
Pollution 9, 47
Population, effect of increased 43
Poultry 11
Prairies 10, 24, 26-27, *26*, 47
Prices, poor harvest and 12
Produce 47
　transporting 9, 23
Productivity, increasing 8
Profits 9

Rancher, ranching 10, 23, 28-29, 47
Range 23
Reclaiming the land 42, *45*, 47
Research 27
Retailers 12, 47
Rice farming *8*, 12, 13, *16*, 41
Rodeo 15, *15*
Rubber 11
Rustlers 29, 47

Scarecrows 18
Scythes 24, 47
Seasons 10-12, 18, 47
　problems for cattle 29
Seed-drills 26
Seeds 9
　failure of 12
　sowing methods 16, 18
Serfs 18, 47
Settlers 20-21, 22, 47
Shaduf 16, *16*, 47
Shearing 31, *30*, 47
Sheep farming 7, 10, 11, 16, *16*, 28, *30*, 31
Sheepdog trials 15
Sickles 24, 47
Single-crop farming 11
Slaves 16, 22
　see also Wage slaves
Smallholders 17, 47
Soil: areas of rich and poor *25*
　infertile 9
Stampedes 23, 47
Steppes 38-39, 47
Stockyards 29
Storms 10, 29
Strip cultivation 18
Subsistence farming 10, 32, 33, 34-35, 36-37, 47
　breakdown of 37
　shared tasks 9, *9*
Sugar 11, 23
　harvest 13

Temperate zones (regions) 10, 47
Tenant farmers 24, 47
Tepees 47
Terracing *8*, 17, 24, 47
Thanksgiving 13
Third World 47
　improving yields *25*
Tools and equipment 9, 10, 24
　invention of new 24
Tractors 24, 26, 32, 43
Trade, development of 7

Vegetables 10, 18

Wage slaves 34-35
Water birds 16
Wheat 7, *6*, 10, 16, 41
　new strains 26
Wholesalers 12, 47
Wigwams *22*, 47

Yield, producing maximum 10
Yurts 38